St Budeaux

St Budeaux
by
Derek Tait

Best wishes,
Derek Tait.

Driftwood Coast Publishing

Frontispiece : The Tomb of St Budoc who died in AD 500.

First published 2007

Driftwood Coast Publishing
PO Box 7, West Park, Plymouth, PL5 2YS.
© Derek Tait, 2007

Contents

Acknowledgements

Thanks to Marshall Ware, Sally Ware, Steve Johnson, Maurice Dart and Michael Isaac.
I have tried to track down the copyright holders of all photos used and apologise to anyone who hasn't been mentioned.
Check out my web pages at : www.derektait.co.uk

Bibliography

Books:
Images of England : Plymouth by Derek Tait (Tempus 2003).
Plymouth at War by Derek Tait (Tempus 2006).
Saltash Passage by Derek Tait (Driftwood Coast 2007).
St Budeaux Yesterday's Village by Marshall Ware (Arthur Clamp 1981).
The Ancient Parish of St Budeaux by Marshall Ware (Arthur Clamp 1983).

Websites:
Brian Moseley's Plymouth Data website at: www.plymouthdata.info
Wikipedia at www,wikipedia.org

Newspapers
Evening Herald
Western Morning News

Driftwood Coast Publishing
© Derek Tait 2007

Introduction

In 480 AD, Budoc, the Bishop of Dol, sailed across from Brittany to the South English coast and landed his craft in an inlet off the River Tamar. This inlet is believed to be at Tamerton Creek. A crude stone cross was erected by him in Ernesettle Woods and a chapel was built near to Warren Point. The original building was just a small wattle church but later, a permanent stone church was built, just before the Norman invasion, and was dedicated to Budoc, The village of St Budeaux is documented in William the Conqueror's Domesday Book of 1086. The area was then known as Bucheside and was valued at 30 shillings which was about 6 times more than the surrounding manors.

Over the next few hundred years, there were various spellings of its name. It became Bodekishide, then Budeokshed and also later, Bottockishide. The name St Budeaux is said to be a later more elegant Frenchification, although after all its name changes, the more modern name isn't far away from the name of it's original founder, St Budoc.

In 1482, the Bishop of Exeter was petitioned by 23 parishioners of St Budeaux church. They requested that the church become a separate parish. The church previously had always been dependant on the monks of St Andrew's for its burials in their cemetery but the trip was hazardous and was a long journey into the centre of Plymouth. The parishioners were granted their request and 40 shillings was paid to St Andrew's for the loss of monies from burials.

In the early Tudor period, there were demands for a bigger church to be built at St Budeaux. It was completed in 1563, five years into the reign of Queen Elizabeth I. It is believed that the money for the building was contributed by Roger Budokshed who owned much of the surrounding

7

land. His family had taken their name from the area. The land was leased by Budokshed to the church for 2000 years with the condition that the yearly amount of one penny was paid between one o'clock and three o'clock on Christmas Day

In 1569, the church saw the marriage of Sir Francis Drake to Mary Newman. It was also involved in a skirmish during the Civil War in the 1600s which left it little more than a wreck. It was restored in 1655.

After the Civil War, the church and the surrounding area reverted back to more peaceful times and any major disputes were settled by the Reverend Thomas Alcock who was described as a loved and respected eccentric.

Until 1850, much of St Budeaux had remained the same for hundreds of years. However, this was all to change with the introduction of the Great Western Railway and the building of the Royal Albert Bridge. Previous to this, the only major development had been the building of Wolseley Road in 1836 which replaced an old track that had been the major riding route between Plymouth and Saltash.

There was later disruption in 1860 when a large part of the land was bought by the War Department for strategic purposes. The Prime Minister of the time, Palmerston, was fearful of a French attack and built many forts in the area. His fears were unfounded though and the forts that scatter the area became known as Palmerston's Folly. However, the change meant a great increase in population which changed the character of the area forever.

In the 1890s, the parish became a self contained village with new shops and better transport. General Trelawny was responsible for much of the redevelopment in Lower St Budeaux after inheriting a large amount of land from his uncle in 1883. The Trelawny family had been the main land owners in the area right back until 1639. In 1890, the General formed the Barne Building Estate, an area that had been gradually growing since the introduction of the railway.

With the opening of its own railway station in 1890 and the tram service being introduced, the village steadily grew and grew. Improvements included new schools, street lighting, paving and a library.

The Second World War caused much devastation to the area. Rebuilding after the war, led to the disappearance of many green areas which made way for new housing.

St Budeaux has certainly had a colourful history and I hope this book will prove interesting to all who have either lived in St Budeaux or have an interest in the area.

One :
Around St Budeaux

George H Ivory, who was a civil engineer in St Budeaux in 1892, stated that they only two inventions that the area benefited from were the railway and the telegraph. He pointed out that there was no resident doctors or health service, that night soil was buried in the back garden and water was hand pumped from individual wells.

St Budeaux, at the time, was thought of as being out in the country. It was classed as being part of Plympton Rural Council and fell in the district of Tavistock Parliamentary Division. When Devonport took over the parish in 1898, they provided a gas and water supply and also an adequate sewerage system.

Millbrook Cottages in 1893. The cottages stood until 1899 when they were demolished to make way for Victoria Road. A young girl leans against a wall to the right of the photo. On the left of the photo, further up the street, is an older woman and a small boy. One of the cottages was inhabited by a Mr Moyle who helped in the construction of the Royal Albert Bridge. Although everything that can be seen in this photo has now gone, it is easy to imagine the line of the road which now takes up part of Victoria Road.

The cottages must have been new in 1846 as Marshall Ware points out in his book, 'St Budeaux Yesterday's Village' , that a notice appeared at the time stating, 'To be let Michaelmas next - four new cottages consisting of three rooms each and a garden. Rent £5 per annum. A portion of land will be let with each cottage if required.' It appears that there are eighteen cottages in this picture so some may have been added on at a later date. The road is unmade and just consists of compressed earth and gravel. The only traffic going up and down it in those days would have been the odd horse and cart making deliveries of coal and other essentials.

The Reverend B J S Vallack and his family at the entrance of the vicarage at Higher St Budeaux. This photo was taken in 1870 and features his wife, four daughters and one son. In 1822, the vicarage was a small cottage with just two rooms on one floor. After he moved in, in 1832, the Reverend Vallack spent a large sum of money and enlarged the building. This was said to be as a thanksgiving for the removal of cholera from the parish. The vicarage fell into disrepair in later years and by the time the Reverend W L Green was appointed in 1886, a new vicarage had been built on the site of where the Cornwall Gate Inn now stands.

Not all of the vicars proved to be popular with their parishioners and on 10th February, 1898, the parish clerk requested that the County Council take action against the Reverent Green and make him hand over to the Parish Council, the tithe map, documents and books. C P Prance of Barne Towers then took control of them.

A more popular vicar was the Reverend T A Hancock who welcomed worshippers to the church in the 1930s. He wrote two booklets, 'St Budeaux Church: Its Documents and Treasures' and 'The Bells of St Budeaux'.

A man and his dog stand in front of what was the last relic of Millbay Cottages in 1899. The jagged edge on the right of the building shows where it had once been joined to the other cottages in the terrace.

The laying of the foundation stone at the Queen Victoria Masonic Hall. This photo was taken on the 8th July, 1899. This was a major event and many people, including children, turned out to see it.

A view of St Budeaux from Barne Farm, in 1893, shows some of the building expansion after the opening of the railway, The Trelawny Hotel can be seen as well as the ancient oak tree. The area has certainly changed and a lot of building work has gone on since this photo was taken over 100 years ago. Barne Barton now stands on the area where this photo is taken from and the fields in the distance now house the expanded estates of St Budeaux and the surrounding areas.

Yeoman's Terrace can be seen to the right of the Trelawny Hotel. This picture shows the houses as people's home but nowadays they are all occupied by shops.

Barne Farm was acquired by the Plymouth Corporation in 1916 to be included in its plans for expansion. In 1935, Moor Farm was also demolished so that new estates could be built. The steadily changing St Budeaux upset many people. The Reverend T A Hancock, who was the vicar at the church at Higher St Budeaux objected to the building plans, He was appalled when the proposal to re-widen Crownhill Road was put forward in the late 1930s. The road cut through his parish and passed right beside the church. Hancock was a well liked vicar and he had a great interest in local history, It was suggested that the road be widened because of the ever increasing traffic in the city and because of the congestion it caused. Hancock wrote in a local paper that widening the road would only invite more traffic to the oldest part of Plymouth. He also said,' Everything we have here will be ruined if the proposals go ahead'. Unfortunately, the Corporation did not take his advice and construction went ahead anyway. Perhaps today's residents of St Budeaux feel the same about the current local planning authorities!

The Methodist Chapel in Tamar Terrace, now Normandy Way, was built in 1893 on a site donated by a Mr Newby Spooner. It was opened on 19th June 1893 by the Reverend W Maltby who gave a sermon at 3.30pm. Tea was also provided at 5pm and tickets were sold at 9d a time.

With the population rising in St Budeaux, and more parishioners seeking places to worship, several other churches were built. These included the Church of St Philip in 1913, St Boniface in 1916 and St Paul's Roman Catholic Church in 1933. Amazingly, before 1885, there was only one church, the church at Higher St Budeaux, to welcome worshippers from the whole parish.

This photo, taken in 1893, shows the interior of the Methodist Chapel. The building has now been taken over by The British Legion.

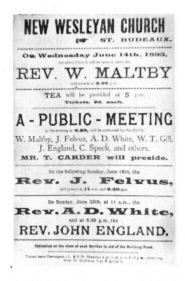

An advert for the New Wesleyan Church announcing its opening on 14th June 1893. A public meeting was held on the first day at 6.30 pm by the Reverends W Maltby, J Felvus, A D White, W T Gill, J England and C Speck. Services were regularly taken by Felvus, White and England. A collection was taken at the close of each service in aid of the building fund.

St Budeaux in the early 1900s. Marshall Ware, who lived at The Kloof in St Budeaux, remembered that the local doctor, Dr Smith, would run a red flag, up a pole in his garden, to let people know that he was out on his rounds and not available to see patients. It's amazing how one doctor in one house would treat nearly all the residents of St Budeaux for their ailments. This practice went on, with doctors operating from houses (I'm sure everyone will remember Dr Norrie at Verna Road) until the 1970s. Now we have surgeries and health centres overflowing with patients. It makes you wonder how the doctors ever coped before.

Marshall Ware also mentioned, regarding the above picture, that Dr Smith's house, which is shown in the photo, was built in 1903 by Dr Smith and his wife, the Honourable Eleanor Smith. It cost £1000 to build and was named, 'Meera'.

Near the railway bridge in the photo, can be seen Mr Cuddeford's milk float. In front of that can be seen the Trelawny Hotel.

The open fields in the background were the venue for the local horse show and the football fields were used by local clubs. A Mr Bradford grew vegetables in some of the fields and he supplied these to, amongst others, the Royal Naval Barracks.

All of the land that you can see in the background of this picture, has now been built on. The old boundary hedges of the farmers' fields can clearly be seen.

Looking at it now, it's hard to imagine that the area was once this open.

A photo of the second vicarage in Vicarage Road. This later became the Cornwall Gate Inn. It was acquired sometime before 1886. Francis Rundle bought the property in 1958 and it was then passed onto H and G Simmonds, who later became Courage, and was then transformed into a Public House.

The Baptist Chapel was opened on the 16th February, 1902. It was built by Tozer and Allen at the bottom of Fletemoor Road, fronting Wolseley Road. Formally, the Baptists had opened a mission in a room above a stable in February 1900. This belonged to Mr Henwood, the local baker, and was situated at the rear of Yeoman's Terrace.

By 1902, there was a congregation of over 200 and 150 children regularly attended Sunday School there.

St Budeaux Square showing the Trelawny Hotel and Yeoman's Terrace. It's strange how this early scene compares with the area today especially with the lack of traffic.

A close up of St Budeaux Square. A few children are sat around a lamp post. The awnings of the shops can be seen in the background. The lamp posts separate the road.

The old bridge at Camel's Head Creek. It was known as Shaky Bridge or the Switch Back. The water from Weston Mill Lake once ran past Barn Quay, through Camel's Head Quay and Lob Quay and up to Weston Mill village. Much of the area has now been reclaimed, partially due to the infamous pong suffered by local residents for many years, and is now used as a parking area.

The condition of the bridge was discussed at a St Budeaux Parish Council meeting in 1897. This was mainly because some of the 12 inch holes that appeared in the structure were a danger to pedestrians and vehicles.

An embankment was built in its place which allowed the Devonport and District Tramway Company to run a through service from Devonport to Saltash Passage.

A scene from the early 1900s of Camels Head showing a Devonport tram heading towards St Budeaux

St Boniface Church at Percy Street. The stone laying ceremony took place on 4th November,1911. The site was given by the Reverend Dr Trelawny Ross of Ham. The church has now been demolished and the congregation meet at a much smaller church built behind where the previous one stood.

St Boniface Church in 1913. A ceremony is taking place watched in the background by two constables. The policemen are Sergeant Wallis and Constable Bawden. Also in attendence are The Bishop of Plymouth, the Lord Mayor and the Reverend H H Ensor who was the vicar of St Boniface.

St Budeaux Church and School at Higher St Budeaux. The area is near to Roman Way which is said to be the way the Romans passed, from their signalling fort at King's Tamerton, on their way to Cornwall.

This photo shows W Tozer's Post Office at Higher St Budeaux in about 1910. It's still easily recognisable today as being the upper end of Victoria Road though the street lamp and the post office are long gone.

Ernesettle Road in 1913. These houses still stand but the land at the far end has now become part of the Devon Expressway leading towards the Tamar Bridge and Cornwall.

The Royal Naval Camp in St Budeaux in 1925. After the First World War, a shore based camp was built called HMS Vivid. This trained stokers, cooks, writers and hands for Naval life. It was called the White City by many locals. Most of this area has now disappeared under subsequent building developments.

The St Budeaux Open Air School for delicate children first opened in November 1920. It was based at Mount Tamar. The children, as can be seen in this picture, would be laid out in the open on beds to take in the fresh air.

Tamar Terrace, St Budeaux. This street was later renamed Normandy Way after the servicemen who passed here on their way to D Day.

Maurice Dart watering plants at his home at Tamar Terrace in the early 1930s.

Morris Park, St. Budeaux

Barne Farm also known as Morris Park. The farm consisted of 168 acres. In the background, can be seen the then new development which included Sithney Street and Colrenick Street. During the 1530s, the farm belonged to the Beele family. The last male heir married the daughter of Jonathan Trelawny of Coldrenick, Menheniot in 1674.The estate was inherited by General J G Trelawny in 1883 and was later sold to the Plymouth Corporation for development.

The Bowling Green. St. Budeaux.

The Bowling Green was situated behind where the library in Victoria Road now stands. On the right of the picture can be seen St Boniface Church A dwindling in the number of worshippers meant that the parish couldn't sustain the cost of such a large church so it has now been demolished.

St Budeaux Square before the building of the Tamar Bridge. On the left can be seen the ancient elm tree planted by General Trelawny. The road leads down to the privately owned shops in Yeoman's Terrace. Older residents may remember Sally Ware, who was a school teacher and lived at the Kloof. She is pictured in the photo wearing a grey coat.

Saltash Passage showing the Royal Albert Bridge and the Mount Edgcumbe Training Ship.

Two:
St Budeaux Church

Two early engravings of the church at Higher St Budeaux. The church looks idyllic in its countryside setting. It's amazing how the area around about has changed over the centuries.

The church was completed in 1563 using land donated by Roger Budokshed. However, remains of an earlier church have been found which is thought to have existed up until 1482. The Norman tympanum (the semi-circle over the doorway) now lies in the church yard.

Perhaps the church at Higher St Budeaux is best known because it is the location of the marriage of Francis Drake to Mary Newman on the 4th July 1569. Francis Drake was the eldest of twelve sons and was born at Tavistock in 1540. He was a distant relative of Sir Walter Raleigh. Mary Newman came from an important St. Budeaux farming and sea-faring family and her father had earlier served with Drake on an attack on the Spanish coast. Drake married Mary Newman before he found fame or wealth. Drake was restless and spent much of his fourteen years of marriage at sea. In 1581, he was knighted by Elizabeth I aboard the Golden Hind.

Drake died of Yellow Fever, age 55, in 1596, on board the Defiance.

The marriage entry from the St Budeaux Church register showing the wedding of Francis Drake to Mary Newman on 4th July, 1569.

There is no proof that Mary Newman ever lived in the dwelling, known as Mary Newman's Cottage, across the water at Culver Road in Saltash. In fact, the story seems to be a concoction to promote tourism and in the 1970s, there were even plans to demolish the building. However, the dwelling is still promoted as the once home to Mary Newman and welcomes visitors from all over the world every year. The only connection the building has with Mary Newman is that it comes from about the same period as when she was alive. Another claim, is that the 16th century farmhouse off Normandy Hill near Saltash Passage was also the dwelling of Mary Newman's family. The building is the right age and should be preserved but it seems that if local builders have their way, it may well be demolished one day.

So little is known about the life of Mary Newman that it will probably be impossible to ever have much more information than that recorded by the parish registers. Her name will always live on though because of her association with Sir Francis Drake.

Sir Francis Drake

Lady Mary Drake died in January 1582 and was buried at the church at Higher St Budeaux but the location of her tomb remains a mystery. The location wasn't known in 1863 so it wouldn't have been amongst those concreted over during building works in 1876.

The entry from the Burial Register from 25th January 1582 which shows an entry for the burial of Lady Mary Drake (nee Newman).

Above the south door of the church is a sundial which was placed there in 1670 and still remains. The wording surrounding it says, 'Ex hoc momento Pendet Aeternitas' which translates to 'From this moment hangs all eternity'.

Used as a garrison in the civil war and left as little more than a wreck after much fighting, the church was restored in 1655.

The Reverend W L Green outside Higher St Budeaux Church. He was appointed in 1886 and lived at the new vicarage which is now the Cornwall Gate Inn. The old vicarage had by then fallen into a state of disrepair. He travelled everywhere in a buggy pulled by a Shetland pony. Famous worshippers at the church, other than Francis Drake, included Lieutenant John Chard VC (of Rourke's Drift fame), Captain Sir Thomas Byard, Lieutenant Commander Malleston VC (Gallipoli Campaigne) and Admiral Sir Peter Richards KCB who was Lord Commissioner of the Admiralty. St Peter's Mission Chapel, which once stood in Saltash Passage, was dedicated to his memory in 1885.

The church itself remains much the same today as it did in Reverend Green's day. The old parts of the graveyard surround the church and newer graves appear outside the church wall but within the church grounds. The church is very close to the busy Crownhill Road. It's hard to imagine how rural and peaceful the area must have been at one time.

Two photos of the interior of Higher St Budeaux Church.

The Altar Tomb.

Three :
The Civil War

Oliver Cromwell

Plymouth and its surrounding villages such as St Budeaux had sworn an oath to fight and die for the Parliamentarian cause. Those who did not comply faced hanging. However, in Cornwall, the people supported the Royalist cause and made raids across the water on parts of St Budeaux. For a time, the church at Higher St Budeaux was used as a garrison by the Royalists. On 16th April 1644, Lieutenant Colonel Martin, who commanded the Parliamentarian garrison at Plymouth, sent 600 musketeers, with 120 horses, to attack the 500 Cavaliers stationed at St Budeaux. Because of a mistake made by guides, the horses went one way and the attacking party went another way. Nevertheless, the foot soldiers arrived at the church, and not being expected, saw off the enemy and captured the church tower. Altogether, they captured 2 officers and 44 other prisoners. They also took three barrels of gunpowder, 20 horses and about 20 arms. It was said that most of the prisoners then joined the Parliament forces and who could blame them when you consider the alternative.

On the 27th December 1644, St Budeaux was again the scene of much bloodshed. From Kinterbury, the Roundheads marched towards the church, which was now a garrison for the Parliamentarians, and fought for an hour and a half before the church was recaptured. The Royalists also captured a Major Stucley together with 20 officers and 100 soldiers. Ten of the defenders were killed as were seven of the Roundheads including a Major Haynes. A mound in a garden at Plaistow, near the church, is said to be the place where those who died in the battle are buried. During the siege of Plymouth by the Royalists, the inhabitants of St Budeaux would take provisions into town for the men and their horses. Prince Maurice issued a warrant which stated, 'To the constables or tythingmen of Saint Budeaux and Pennyross, threatening proceedings against all who should carry with him horse, oxen or kine, or sheep or other provision for men or horse into the said town of Plymouth for the relief of the rebells there.'

After the battle, the church was little more than a wreck and it wasn't restored until 1655.

Interestingly, when the old Crownhill Road was widened in 1910, several cannon balls were found in the hedges. Undoubtedly, many still remain there to this day.

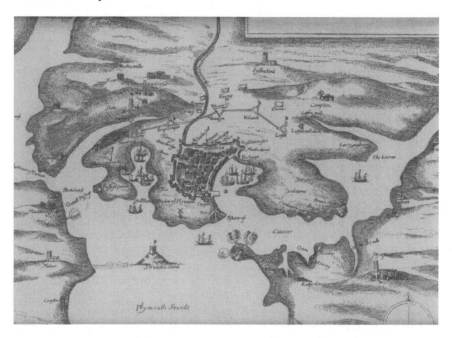

A map from the Civil War showing the land around St Budeaux marked in the top left hand corner as St Butoks. Nearby is Saltash Passage, Ham, 'Weston Mills' , 'Penicross' and 'Egbucland'. It's interesting to see how these names have evolved over the years. Enemy locations are also marked on the map particularly in the area then known as 'Penycomquic'. The darker area towards the middle of the map, shows 'Charles Fort' complete with drawbridge.

The old Crownhill Road where cannonballs were discovered in the hedges in 1910. The church can be seen on the left of the picture which also features the St Budeaux Inn.

A view looking up towards the church.

Four :
The People

Rabbit hunting was a popular pastime which involved many local people who would bring their dogs and ferrets. This outing in 1898 features a military man, probably from the local camp.

This photograph, taken in 1895, shows a St Budeaux Parish councillor with his family. It shows one of the slip bar and swing gates that were provided for pedestrians on local footpaths. There were protests when Government authorities removed many of these from the area. The last swing gate, stile and granite slip bar was at Little Ash Farm in Saltash Passage until 1920.

A group assembled for the opening of the new rifle range in 1913. In the front row is N Bucknell (a schoolmaster at Victoria Road School), a Mrs Thomas (who was the wife of Dr Thomas) and Tom Occleshaw, the local barber.

All babies were delivered by local midwives in the St Budeaux area. Granny Uren was one such midwife and is shown here with her daughter, her grand daughter and her great grand daughter. She was well respected and known for her caring manner. The first local doctor in the area, a Dr Smith, left all the midwifery duties to her.

Ladies of Lower Saint Budeaux all shown here in their Sunday best complete with hats.

A gent somewhere in St Budeaux with his horse and buggy carrying his family.

Here's a photo of Mr Whiteford standing beside the Barne Lane toll gate. Mr Whiteford was the driver of Cuddeford's milk float. Barne Lane stretches from Trelawny Place to Victoria Road.

Gladys Cuddeford at Barne Farm in 1912.Her horse was later taken for the First World War. So many horses were needed in the War, for both transport and cavalry charges, that over eight million died. Two and a half million were successfully treated by vets of which two million returned to service. It's very unlikely that Gladys ever saw her horse again.

Mr Cleave's haulage horse shown here at Camel's Head. The St Budeaux Horse show drew in entries from as far away as Totnes and Liskeard. The annual event was very popular and was supported by local tradesmen and farmers. The judges of the event were put up at the nearby Trelawny Hotel. From 1910 onwards, General Stone of Mount Tamar was the chairman. Mr R Luscombe, of Warleigh, Tamerton, was a local breeder of horses and won many awards at the event.

James Ware's Coal Carts proudly displayed at a local show. James Ware owned Ware's Quay at Saltash Passage and used it until 1922.

The St Budeaux Regatta, here showing a float sponsored by J Cleave and Son of Devonport. The event had much support from local shopkeepers and businesses and many church groups took part.

Shown here is one of James Ware's prized horses. The cart was made by Edward Petherick of Weston Mill. Boxer won a blue rosette at the St Budeaux Horse Show in 1912. A car park (now gone) stood on the site of the station yard for many years. In the background, can be seen Yeoman's Terrace which is now part of the shopping centre at St Budeaux Square.

Kinterbury Villa football team seen here in 1923. They were one of St Budeaux's local teams and won the Junior League Cup in the same year that this picture was taken. Painted on their football is, 'K V A FC 1922 - 23'.They disbanded in 1924.

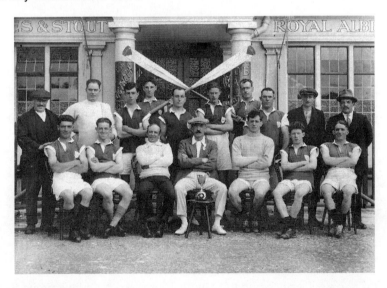

A local football team shown in September 1925 outside the Royal Albert Bridge Inn in Saltash Passage. The team are holding crossed oars in the background which may signify which team they played for. The man in the centre, wearing a cloth cap, has a trophy proudly displayed in front of him. The photo was taken by Quick and Son of Saltash.

The St Boniface Church Club shown here in 1928 wearing their tasselled berets. Before the Second World War, many churches had their own rowing clubs for young people.

The St Budeaux Baptists and their boat. Swimming from their boats was a popular pastime. The swimming costumes have certainly changed over the years!

The St Boniface Boating Club shown here in 1928.Some members of boat clubs took their gramophone players with them on their boat. The only problem they had, apart from the weight, was that their records sometimes buckled in the Summer heat.

Maurice Dart shown holding a ball in 1937. Maurice remembers that this picture was taken within Higher St Budeaux Recreation Grounds. Although 70 years ago, Maurice remembers the ball well which he remembers as being very bouncy and coloured blue, yellow and red.

Five :
Transport

Edmund Tolley was the first stationmaster at St Budeaux station in 1890. He was well liked and was remembered for holding up the trains for latecomers.

The station was originally known as St Budeaux Platform and opened on the 1st June, 1904. It was built by the Great Western Railway. It was a busy stopping off place and in 1906, because of its popularity, the platforms were widened and a new ticket office and waiting room was built.

Between 1913 and 1937, there were four staff employed at the station. The station was named Ferry Road in 1948 so there was no confusion between it and Victoria Road Station in the Southern Region.

A goods train that was derailed in 1892 near to St Budeaux. The driver was killed in the accident and sabotage was suspected. In the background can be seen an ancient elm tree which was removed in 1928.

An early shot of St Budeaux train station taken in the late 1800s. Much of the station has now changed. The shelters on the right have disappeared as have the seating and the lampposts.

As well as the stationmaster, Edmund Tolley, the St Budeaux station had a staff of three other people, two of who can be seen in this picture waiting for the arrival of the next train.

A goods train on the St Budeaux line. Here, the 7209 with its six carriages passes under the bridge near Wolseley Road.

Motor Train

This picture was taken on 26th August 1906. The two coach motor trains running to Millbay Station were a common site at one time. The fare to Plymouth from St Budeaux was 3d return.

Sailors waiting at Victoria Road Station.

St Budeaux station when it was still known as Victoria Road sometime prior to 1948.

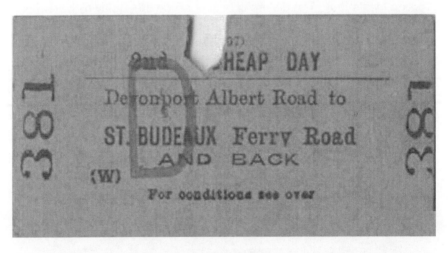

A cheap day return rail ticket from Albert Road, Devonport to Ferry Road, St Budeaux.

This early photo shows one of the annual outings of the St Budeaux Working Men's Club. The picture is taken outside the Trelawny Hotel.

A charabanc outing setting off from St Budeaux in the1920s. Charabancs were very popular during the 1920s. Many trips were works outings and visited places such as Dartmoor, Mount Edgcumbe, Cawsands and Saltash Passage.

Six :
Businesses

Mrs Cann delivering milk in St Budeaux. She is pictured here in Coldrenick Street during the First World War. She is helped by her daughter, Mrs Doidge. Milk wasn't delivered in bottles then but was measured out from a churn on the back of the cart.

A gathering outside the Trelawny Hotel which was built by Major General John Jago Trelawny in 1895. The first landlord was a Joseph Striplin who was then followed by Harry Hearn.

This butcher's cart belongs to Mr C Robertshaw and is shown here in 1892. Mr Robertshaw was the only butcher delivering to the area from his nearby premises in Ford. Two ladies collect their meat for the week, pictured in Edith Street on either a Tuesday or Thursday, which were the two days that Mr Robertshaw delivered to St Budeaux. It's interesting to see the two boys on the left of the picture enthralled by what is going on. Photography would have been a relatively new invention and people would gather whenever photos were taken.

Tom Occleshaw's shop in Yeoman's Terrace was a hairdressers and tobacconists. Yeoman's Terrace in now situated in St Budeaux Square and forms part of the shops still there today. The shop was formally Mr Occleshaw's home but it was converted into a shop in 1901. To start off with, it was just lit by oil lamps but later on it was the first shop to be lit by gas lighting. Tom Occleshaw's son, Sidney, carried on the business and also sold sweets and tobacco. Robin Occleshaw ran the business when Sidney died but the Occleshaw name disappeared from the shop in 1980 when it was sold to another trader. Other shops in Yeoman's Terrace included a boot makers opened by a Mr Truscott and a dairy ran by the Menheneotts. Mr Blackmore sold butter and cream from 1 Yeoman's Terrace and there was also a general shop ran by a Mr Eastlake.

Another shot of Occleshaw's showing more of Yeoman's Terrace. From this view, it's possible to see where the row of shops stand today.

The Plymouth Co-operative Society bought Stuart House in Trelawny
Road on 1st October, 1895. It cost them £900 and they had it converted
into a butcher's and grocery store at a cost of £339.
When it opened on the 1st December, 1895, a Mr W Shepherd was the
first manager followed by a Mr A D Hammett in 1901.His staff consisted of
two assistants and one apprentice. The apprentice would have been paid
twelve shillings for a sixty hour week. Here, they are assembled outside
the shop wearing their aprons.

Seven :
The Blue Monkey

An early engraving from the 1800s showing Higher St Budeaux with St Budeaux Church on the left and St Budeaux Inn (later the Blue Monkey) on the right.

Although the public house has now been knocked down, the area near to the Higher St Budeaux Church will probably always be known as the Blue Monkey. It had previously been called Church Inn, St Bude Inn, St Budeaux Inn and Ye Old St Budeaux Inn before becoming the Blue Monkey. The owner of the Church Inn was a Lord Graves who owned the Barton of Ernesettle in 1798. He was also Lord of the Manor of Agaton. Frances Martin is recorded as being the landlord of the pub in 1823. He was responsible for changing the pub's name to the St Bude Inn, in 1828. In 1862, the War Department bought the then named St Budeaux Inn.

In 1914, the Secretary of State for the Department sold the premises, which included a stables, to James Alger for £1,050. Alger changed the name of the pub to Ye Old St Budeaux Inn on 4 May 1937. He later changed the name again to The Blue Monkey early in 1939 and later sold the Inn to the Octagon Brewery in December 1939 for £12,750.

A newspaper cutting that used to hang in the bar said that a Mr Dunsford, the then landlord, changed the name to the Blue Monkey when the Stafford Regiment was stationed at Devonport. However, the deeds say that the name was changed in 1939 by James Algar. The reason, according to locals, was that Algar had seen a monkey which had escaped from a shed at Agaton on the roof of the Inn.

Apparently, the change of name and the swinging monkey sign wasn't popular, even though it's the one best remembered, so it was replaced by a square sign , featuring a Naval Blue Monkey Boy, in honour of the boys who packed the guns with powder during the Battle of Trafalgar in 1805. They were known as powder monkeys and the job left them with blue residue on their hands and this has also been taken as the origin of the pub's name, The Blue Monkey. Perhaps both stories are true and it would be interesting to think that a monkey once ran around on the roof of the Inn.

Incidently, before the sign change, in the early 1980s, I was walking by the Inn and there was the swinging monkey sign, slightly battered and put out for the dustbin men to collect. I wish I'd picked it up and kept it as a souvenir now! I wonder if it still exists somewhere?

In its final years, the Inn got a bad reputation and finally closed and was eventually bricked up. It was for sale for many years before an arson attack destroyed the inside and the roof. From then on, its days were numbered and early in March 2007 it was unfortunately demolished.

This photo shows the pub as it was when it was still the Old St Budeaux Inn before it was renamed the Blue Monkey.

Eight: Schools

When the Admiralty School at Bull Point closed down in 1900, the Devonport School Board met to decide what was to be done with the 150 to 200 children that had attended. Added to this figure were another 200 children who were already receiving no schooling at all. The Masonic Hall could hold 100 children but the sanitary conditions weren't seen as fit for the purpose. The Baptist Mission room was also considered unsuitable. The Chairman of the School Board thought it unwise for the Admiralty to close the school at the time but the Reverend S G Ponsonby suggested that even if the school was to remain open it couldn't possibly cope with the numbers of children that needed to attend.

The School Board purchased an acre and a quarter of land. At first, the plan was to just erect a one storey building which would open in 1901 to be used as a boys' school and then later, when a two storey building could be added, this would house the girls and the infants.

When completed, the school was officially known as the Devonport Victoria Road Board School. Pupils were told to register on 31st December 1900 at the Masonic Hall as the buildings for the new school hadn't been completed.

On 7th April 1902, the Reverend W Mantle, chairman of the school board, officially opened the new school building in Trelawney Avenue. Other members of the board, Reverend S G Ponsonby and Mr W Garstang were also in attendance.

Once the school was opened, Mr Phipps, the teacher for the mixed school and Miss Moore, the teacher for the infants school, opened the register to record the names of the children who wished to attend. These included 270 boys and 150 infants. The building could house double that amount. It was thought that the girls were allowed to apply at a later date so the numbers of pupils would have been a lot greater than recorded.

The cost of the school was £11,000 and it was built by W E Blake of Plymouth. There were 10 class rooms and two cloakrooms on each of the two floors. The ground floor housed the infants and the first floor housed the mixed school of older children. Outside, was a large plot used as a playground and also another plot of ground to be used if the school had to expand.

A class at the St Budeaux Foundation School, shown in 1895. The charity school was opened on the green near the Church Inn (later the Blue Monkey) in 1717. It housed six poor girls and six poor boys from the Parish of St Budeaux. At the time, there were few schools and many children went uneducated.

The class of Miss Bonney, seen on the right of the picture. This photo taken at the Foundation School probably dates from about 1905. The headmaster at the time would have been Mr Joseph Warring who held the position between 1883 and 1923.

St Budeaux Parish Church Sunday School taken in the early 1900s. All are dressed well and many of the girls are wearing bonnets.

This photo shows local children at Victoria Road School in 1905. An '8' has been chalked on the board held by the boy in the front row probably making this class 8. I wonder how many of their descendants still live in St Budeaux?

In 1896, when the school at Bull Point closed, the boys were sent to the Masonic Hall where Edgar Phipps was in charge. The girls went to the Wesleyan Chapel in the care of a Miss Bailey. The children were moved to the Victoria Road School in 1902 and Mr Phipps became headmaster.

Class 5 at Victoria Road School. Miss Ida Worth was the teacher. Miss Worth can be seen to the right of the picture and Miss Fuller is on the left.

Another old photo featuring the children of Victoria Road School.

Children in Mr Norman Bucknell's class, also at Victoria Road School. Some of the children in this class of older boys are wearing school uniforms and one boy is wearing a striped blazer. The cost of a uniform might have been hard to find at the time and some children are just dressed in their best clothes, though many wear ties.

The staff of Victoria Road School. In this photo are, in the back row, Miss L Packer, Mr E Petherick, Mr H N Bucknell, Mr T Garland and Mr L Williams. In the front row are Miss D Teppett, Miss Little, Mr N Phipps (the headmaster), Miss I Worth, Miss H Woods and Miss Fuller.

The class of Miss Ingram at the St Budeaux Foundation School. Miss Ingram can bee seen at the back of the room. This photo was probably taken in the 1930s.

Children in fancy dress for the Silver Jubilee of 1935. The boys at the back are dressed as guards with home made shields and spears.

An early shot showing the St Budeaux Foundation School on the left and the church at Higher St Budeaux on the right. The road leading down was a lot quieter in those days. The fields in the foreground have, for many years, had houses built on them.

Ewart Prior, headmaster at the St Budeaux Foundation School between 1933 and 1940.

A class photo from 1937 showing Ewart Pryor, the headmaster. Mr Pryor was the great grandson of Joseph Pryor who had also been headmaster at the school almost 100 years before. Mr Aubrey Pryor, Ewart Pryor's elder brother, became headmaster in 1946 and stayed until he retired in 1961. Ewart Pryor was awarded the MBE in 1946 and the OBE in 1947. He was very popular with the children and staff and was said to have a good sense of fun.

Another photo showing Mr Ewart Pryor with Miss Ingram's class in 1937. Maurice Dart is in the middle row, third from the left.

Ewart Pryor pictured with Miss Packer's class in 1939. Maurice Dart is in the back row, second from the left.

The school was the first to have railings, at the pavement's edge, after a girl from the school, aged 7, ran out and was knocked down and killed in 1936.

Nine :
During the Second World War

St Budeaux suffered in the Second World War mainly due to its proximity to the Dockyard, the Royal Albert Bridge and the nearby armaments dump. All were major targets for the invading Luftwaffe.

The view that the Luftwaffe would have got of the Royal Albert Bridge as they flew over St Budeaux. There were several attempts to bomb the bridge and the armaments depot behind but all proved fruitless. However, an armaments barge was hit on the River Tamar which caused devastation to the nearby Saltash Passage.

Here is a photo of Barne Towers. It was destroyed by enemy action in 1941. It was the home for many years of Cecil P Prance who, in 1894, was the chairman of St Budeaux Parish Council. On the Western edge of the property, stood the boundary stone for Cornwall. The site is now occupied by a petrol station.

Just before the start of the Second World War, the St Budeaux cinema company was formed in March 1939. They had a capital of £10,000 which was all in £1 shares. Perhaps if the cinema had been proposed further into the war, it might not have been built due to the lack of materials and resources.

On 16th October, 1939, a month into the war, the State Cinema opened at the junction of Victoria Road and Stirling Road. It seated 1,000 people and was the first cinema in Plymouth to be fitted with a four channel stereophonic system.

The first film shown was 'That Certain Age' starring Deanna Durbin and Melvyn Douglas. The seats were 6d, one shilling and 1/6d. There were two shows daily. The cinema was certainly popular and queues would form right around it when a new film was shown.

It escaped the bombing during the war and unfortunately closed in 1983. It still stands though, in later years, it has become a carpet warehouse and a snooker hall.

A 1940s view towards the Royal Albert Bridge. This would have been taken from land that now forms part of Barne Barton.

A direct hit on a house at Higher St Budeaux. It's possible to see areas of bomb damage all over Plymouth. In parts, houses have been rebuilt, sometimes in a different style, but in other places there are just large gaps between terraces.

A girl recovering her belongings from a bombed house in St Budeaux. Anything that could be saved would be put to use as there was a shortage of even the most basic items.

All that remains of a house after a bombing raid. During a raid in the area
on 28th August, 1940, six bombs and several incendiaries were dropped
in the countryside between St Budeaux and Crownhill. Incendiaries were
quickly dealt with by the Auxiliary Fire Service.

St Budeaux Station on April 1941 which appears to be just before the
bombing raids of that month.

Passengers waiting for a train at Victoria Road Station during the war. A couple of people can be seen carrying their gas masks.

A close up shot of the passengers waiting on the platform at the St Budeaux Station. In the background can be seen adverts for Lidstones of the Octagon and also one for Moon's Pianos.

The waiting room at St Budeaux station after a bomb raid during 1941. Advertising signs of the day show adverts for Virol (which was a dietary supplement for children), Swan Vesta Matches and the Cornish Times. Several tiles are missing and the building beside has had its roof destroyed by the blast.

A photo showing people getting food from the Queen's Messengers' Convoy lorry. St Budeaux was once served by two railway stations. The one above was situated in the middle of the busy junction near St Budeaux Square where Victoria Road meets Wolseley Road and Trelawney Place.

Shown above are the remains of the west signal box foundations after a raid on St Budeaux. On the 28th April 1941, the bombing raids centred mainly on St Budeaux, Bull Point, Camels Head and Devonport. There were 42 fires caused by the raid but the damage caused wasn't as extensive as raids on the city on previous nights. A new signal box was opened on 5th November 1941 but it had a short life and was closed on the 22nd June 1952 when its operations were transferred to the Royal Albert Bridge Signal Box.

The American base at Vicarage Road. The Royal Albert Bridge can be seen in the background. The Americans arrived in Saltash Passage early in 1944. Local residents realised something was going on when a construction firm built a huge oil tank on Little Ash Farm. The Americans took over the Vicarage (now the Cornwall Gate Inn) and were stationed at the camp at Vicarage Road (now Normandy Hill).

Maurice Dart remembers the American soldiers who were stationed here before D Day. He also recalls their generosity.

Maurice remembers: 'We would go down to the gate sometimes and they would give us chocolates and sweets and items to take home such as tins of cocoa, biscuits and butter. My mother used to tell me off for scrounging but she was always glad to receive it all!'

At the time, the Americans weren't restricted by rationing unlike the British.

A unit of the 456th Battalion were stationed at Woodland Fort and part of the unit guarded the camp at Vicarage Road and also guarded the Royal Albert Bridge. Many of them became friends with the locals. Saltash Passage residents all had ID cards but were issued with an extra yellow Certificate of Residence Card. It proved that the owner lived in the area and was issued because of the secrecy building up to the D Day landings. On 6th June 1944, local residents awoke to find the area unusually quiet and found the Forces had gone leaving only a baseball bat which was kept as a souvenir by Graham Langston who was the Unigate milkman in the area.

Many local people have fond memories of the Americans. Unfortunately, many lost their lives on the beaches of Normandy.

VE Day at Saltburn Road. It seems strange that this picture consists of mainly women and children but all of the younger male members of the community were probably away serving in the forces.

VE day celebrated the Victory in Europe of the Allied Forces. Germany surrendered on the 7th May 1945 and the end of the war was declared on Tuesday 8th May 1945. Winston Churchill announced the end of the war in a broadcast on the radio. The news was met with relief, sadness, pride and celebration. However, the war was not over and battles still raged in the Far East with the Japanese forces.

In his speech Churchill paid tribute to the men and women who had laid down their lives for victory as well as to all those who had fought valiantly on land, sea and in the air.

There was much jubilation at the announcement of the end of the war in Europe and there were many street parties held on VE Day. Streets were filled with trestle tables, chairs and bunting. Thousands of people turned out all over the country to celebrate.

Local residents celebrated as much as anyone. Plymouth had seen its fair share of bombing and St Budeaux hadn't gone unscathed. Rations had been saved up for this day and their were sandwiches and cakes galore especially for the children who had been deprived of sweets and treats during the war.

Ten :
After the War

This photo shows the Eagles cycling team from Barne Barton in 1950. Speedway cycling was once very popular in the area and the team had an incredible following. Local rivals included the Ernesettle Boars. In the background can be seen the old prefabs built to house people after the war.

Victoria Road in the 1950s. Little has changed here except there is now a lot more traffic on the road. A couple of old cars can be seen in the picture as well as a very old fashioned looking road bollard on the right. In the background can be seen the River Tamar.

Alan Tait at Barne Barton park in the late 1950s. The park is still there but everything shown here has long gone including the concrete steam train and the millstone seating area.

A man fiddles with a petrol lawn mower in the background and parents push their children on the swings. The men are all wearing cloth caps.

The building of the Tamar Bridge shown here in May 1960. The road bridge opened on the 24th October, 1961. It cost £1,345,556 to build.

A 1960s photo of the ferry at Saltash Passage. A Ford Anglia is just about to drive off. Also on the ferry is a removal lorry belonging to McMullins. A mother waits with her two sons who are dressed for school.
This photo may show the last day of the ferry, in October 1961, as the Tamar road bridge can be seen in the background. A Union Jack is being flown at the other end of the ferry.

A 1970s/1980s shot of the St Budeaux Foundation Church of England Junior School. The school was founded in 1717 but was knocked down, to make way for the access to the Tamar Bridge, in the early 1980s.
The school was originally situated on the village green but was re-sited in 1876. Two of the last teachers at the school included Mr Rodney Dart, the headmaster and Mr John Finch, the deputy headmaster.

Here's a picture of the school house adjoining the school. It too has now been demolished but many people will remember the unusual building with its ornamental wishing well, wheel barrow and wheels on the walls.

Eleven :
St Budeaux Today

Much of old St Budeaux still exists. The Trelawny Hotel and the shops at the old Yeoman's Terrace still form part of St Budeaux Square. The area has become far more busy now though, not just with people but with the constant stream of traffic. The area isn't too different though and it's still possible to recognise a lot of the old buildings featured in many of the photos in this book. Victoria Road leading from the Square to Higher St Budeaux is still laid out much the same as it was at the beginning of the last century though shops have come and gone and some new buildings and houses have appeared off the main road mainly in the Sterling Road area. The State Cinema building is still there though a bit run down and looking worse for wear. Maybe this could be said for a lot of the commercial buildings in the area.

Further towards the Tamar, travelling along Normandy Way, the houses on the right that were once Tamar Terrace, still stand. There are newer houses on the left but even these are gathering age now. The Cornwall Gate Inn, formally the Vicarage, still stands and serves customers.

Heading down towards Saltash Passage, it's possible to see some of the old buildings that have been there for over a hundred years and also the magnificent Royal Albert Bridge.

Barne Barton remains much the same as it did in the 1950s though a few new housing developments have sprung up.

Heading towards Higher St Budeaux, the Blue Monkey Pub has now unfortunately gone. Just behind it though, is the church at Higher St Budeaux where Francis Drake was married. This remains pretty much the same as it did several hundred years ago.

St Budeaux Square with the Trelawny Hotel on the left and the shops at Yeoman's Terrace nearby.

A present day view of the Trelawny Hotel with regulars outside taking a smoking break. The hotel has certainly seen many changes over the years and is no longer the place it once was. It's still instantly recognisable though from old photos of it from the turn of the 20th Century.

St Budeaux station. Now somewhat run down, there seems to be few travellers there at the best of times. It almost has an eerie feeling about it now and I certainly wouldn't want to be getting on or off a train there at night time!

The rail line approaching the Royal Albert Bridge. The busy road bridge is in the background.

The Cornwall Gate Inn. Like the Trelawny Hotel, the Cornwall Gate Inn has seen better days too. A lot of business would have been lost when the road traffic to the bridge was diverted along the Parkway back in the 1980s.

Normandy Way, once Tamar Terrace, renamed after the America servicemen who passed by this way in 1944 on their way to the D Day landings.

The Methodist Chapel Hall, now the British Legion, which incorporates the house beside it.

The top of Victoria Road. It's easy to imagine this scene as it was fifty years ago as little has changed.

The Blue Monkey Pub unfortunately being demolished in March 2007.

The church at Higher St Budeaux.
From this angle, little appears to have changed for hundreds of years. The old sundial can just be seen above the church door. This is one part of old St Budeaux that remains and is well worth a visit.

95

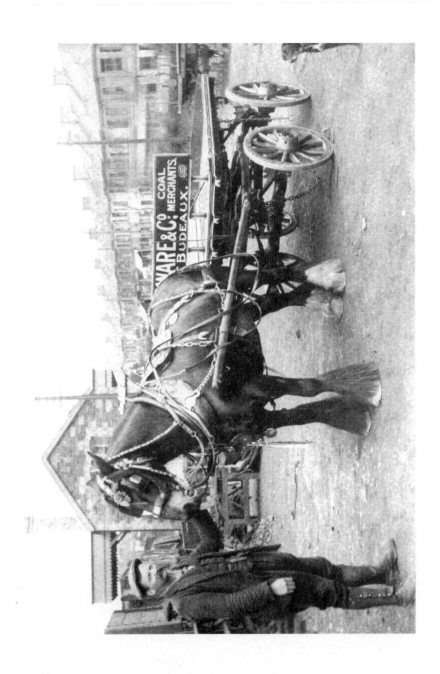

97

TAMOR TERRACE. ST. BUDEAUX.

A 7272.

99

~ St Budeaux Church & School ~

The Bowling Green. St. Budeaux. A 1922.

By the same author :

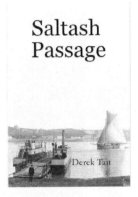

Saltash Passage

A history of Saltash Passage, Plymouth. Contains over 140 old photos
and illustrations.
104 pages.
Price : £9.99.
ISBN-13: 978-0955427732.

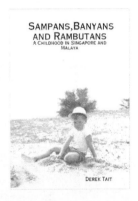

Sampans, Banyans and Rambutans
A Childhood in Singapore and Malaya

A childhood spent in Singapore and Malaya in the 1960s as part of a
Naval family.
104 pages.
Price : £7.99.
ISBN-13: 978-0955427701.

Memories of Singapore
and Malaya

Derek Tait

Memories of Singapore and Malaya

Memories of Singapore and Malaya during the 1950s,1960s and 1970s
through the eyes of servicemen and their families.
Contains 230 photos.
194 pages.
Price : £9.99.
ISBN-13: 978-0955427756.

Available from all good bookshops.
Signed copies are available from
Derek Tait, PO Box 7, West Park, Plymouth, England, PL5 2YS.
Postage and packing on all books within the UK is £1.50.

Further copies of this book can be also obtained from the above address
for £9.99.

Driftwood Coast Publishing